HOLIDAY FUN!

EASTER

by Adeline J. Zimmerman

I0804565

TABLE OF CONTENTS

tadpole books

WORDS TO KNOW

basket

bunny

chocolate

dye

lily

meal

EASTER

I see a bunny!

egg

I see dye.

I see a basket.

I see chocolate.

I see a meal.

I see a lily.

I see eggs!

LET'S REVIEW!

A holiday is a special day. Easter is in spring. How is this family celebrating?

INDEX